S0-ALN-417

A Single Mother, A Few Perspectives... And anyone else that is a Single Parent

By

MARY ELIZABETH JONES M.A

5/13

Copyright © 2012 Mary Elizabeth Jones M.A

All rights reserved.

ISBN: 1479352071

ISBN 13: 9781479352074

Library of Congress Control Number:2012917724
CreateSpace Independent Publishing Platform
North Charleston, South Carolina

To my mother, Sylvia Mines, Barbara, Delia, Kameelah, Myron, Charlie, Jason Lucas Sr., Jason Lucas Jr., Sonny, Jason Mines, Asya, and Createspace.

Thank you for your love, support, and inspiration. Without you all, this book would not have been possible for single parents.

Disclaimer:

This book describes the author personal experiences coping with single parenthood. Although every effort has been made to ensure the accuracy of the contents of this book, errors, and omissions may occur. The author or publisher assumes no responsibility for any damages arising from the use of this book, or alleged to have resulted in connection with this book.

This book is not completely comprehensive. Some reader may wish to consult additional resources if the need should arise, or when appropriate.

The company mentioned throughout this book does not pay the author or publisher any endorsements or provide any funding whatsoever.

A Single Mother: A Few Perspectives

… and anyone else who is a single parent

Table of Contents

Words from the author

When you hear the term "single mother," what is the first thing that comes to mind? Is it poverty, welfare, struggle, or simply taboo? There are many negative stereotypes regarding the single mother. Single motherhood affects women of all races and backgrounds, regardless of their circumstances — whether those women are divorced, widowed, never been married, or was single by choice. Being a single mother is an epidemic that grows every second of the day. The following are some alarming statistics regarding single motherhood.

According to the US Census Bureau in November 2009:

- There are approximately 13.7 million single parents in the United States, and those parents are responsible for raising 21.8 million children (approximately 26 percent of children under the age of twenty-one in the US today).
- Approximately 84 percent of custodial parents are mothers; and 16 percent of custodial parents are fathers.
- Of the mothers who are custodial parents, 45 percent are currently divorced or separated, 34.2 percent have never been married, 19 percent are married (in most cases, these numbers represent women who have remarried), and 1.7 percent were widowed.

It is obvious how a child is created, and most importantly, it is a mother—who gives that child life, regardless of the consequences. A number of women did not realize that they were going to be a single mother (including myself) until they received their pregnancy results. When that happens, you realize that you are no longer able to think of only about "you" in all aspects of your life.

Single motherhood may very well be hard at times, but the crucial part about it is this, and please read carefully: The decisions you make each and every day of your life (and in your child's or children's lives) will make being a single mother a more fulfilling role.

This book focuses on ways to improve single motherhood. There are so many stereotypical and negative views out there on the nature of single motherhood, and I strongly believe it is best to maneuver away from that viewpoint. Therefore, areas such as custody disputes, deadbeat fathers, liars, cheaters, violence, or anything pertaining to abuse or drugs **will not be found within this book.** Instead, you will find ways to make extra money each month, several tactics to make that money grow within five to ten years (or sooner), one way in particular to find your "dream" and implement it, and methods to balance your life by eliminating stress. This book only focuses on ways the single mother could get further in life on an emotional, financial, and educational level. Any advice given in this book is exclusively meant to encourage, and is based on either personal experience or scholarly evidence. It is not intended to offend anyone in any way whatsoever.

Introduction

I was born with Blount's disease (a muscle disorder). I currently stand at four feet ten inches without shoes. I was raised in a two-parent middle-class home. My parents were married for twenty-five years. I have three sisters. Both my mother and father held good jobs. Our family never received welfare assistance. However, we lived in the inner city with a poor school system. I firmly believe a child can potentially become a product of his or her environment. If a school system is rated poor in academics based on state standards, what are the children inside those buildings focused on and learning? I loathe bringing this up, but these children are most likely cutting classes to have sex to participate in many other activities that would hurt or anger their parents. However, there are a small number of students that skip school for positive reasons, such as to go to the library to study for a difficult exam.

When I was a teen, I hung out with the wrong group of girls, and I became pregnant at the age of fourteen. My father was furious with me that I had disobeyed him, and since I had strayed away from his teachings, he encouraged me to have an abortion so that my pregnancy would become an "out of sight, out of mind" occurrence. He constantly reminded me that my life would become nothing but an eternal hell if I decided to have my baby. But even at the tender age of fourteen, and not knowing how to proceed with this situation, I just knew one thing: my child deserved to have a life just like I did. The father of my child was young as well—he was fifteen and just wanted to have fun hanging out with his friends. I could not call on him for any type of financial or moral support, but I was not upset with him. It was my decision to keep the child, and the hard realization of the matter was that I particularly needed my mother's help. Since I was too young to support myself.

Throughout the duration of my pregnancy, my father became extremely ill, and one month after my son was born, my father died.

Three months later, my mother moved my sisters and me to the suburbs to expose us to a better way of life, a better school system, and a cleaner environment without the high crime rates, vacant buildings, and trashed streets. My mother helped with my son significantly while I tried my best to focus on schoolwork. When I reached the age of sixteen, it wasn't long before I met someone at a summer party; it became an exclusive sexual relationship for a few years.

When I entered college, this guy and I became boyfriend and girlfriend. I really fell head over heels for him. I didn't have to worry about an apartment for the first two years of college since his home was my home. By the time I got to my junior year in college, I became pregnant with his child. I told him that I was keeping it, and he left.

I finished college with a Bachelor's Degree in Family Consumer Sciences at Kent State University and earned a Master's Degree in Management and Leadership from Liberty University. Over time to help with stress, I became a writer who enjoy discussing and providing deeper insight into interesting topics and sharing these topics with all sorts of readers.

The goal of this book is to present single motherhood in a more positive light than it usually is, regardless of one's situation. To help you understand this better, consider my story; instead of being upset at the outcome, over time, I decided to learn how to use my energy in a positive way to improve myself for my children. Energy is such an important characteristic of human beings that it is easily taken for granted on a daily basis. From talking and thinking to making decisions, it all takes energy, so why not use that energy in a positive way? After all, you have control over it.

CHAPTER 1

Now You Are a Single Mother: A Few Directions to Look Forward To

Life is simply what you make it. - Anonymous

Mothers in today's society are becoming younger and younger. I have personally met and talked to pregnant females as young as eleven years old. Although I was a teenage mother once, I do not condone teenage pregnancy. It is a reality of life that must be dealt with and discussed. The information throughout this book must be used accordingly.

In other words, a thirteen-year-old single mother could and should not use the same advice that would be given to a twenty-three or thirty-three–year-old mother. But no need to worry, there will be informational pieces for both types of single mothers, since each is still an unmarried female with a child.

A female who is fifteen years old or younger and who is expecting a baby or already has a child has **extremely limited** financial options. Of course, there is the option of babysitting a local neighbor's child or children to earn money, and

1

this offers some overall parenting experience. But this will not provide a stable income to support a child. The government offers some programs for teenage mothers. These programs include:

- LEAP (Learning, Earning, and Parenting) - Teen parents under the age of nineteen who are on OWF (Ohio Works First Cash Support) and who come back or stay in school to generate a qualification or G.E.D are offered childcare through this system. If certain specifications are met, members get a supplement through their current OWF check, and if the specifications **are not** met, their OWF check will be sanctioned. (This program is for Ohio residents only. Check your local county for a similar program.) **Source: http://www.childtrends.org/Lifecourse/ programs/OhioLEAP.htm**

- WIC (Women, Infants, and Children) – This program provides coupons for certain healthy foods such as bread, juice, and milk, and provides information about nutrition for expectant mothers and children up to five years of age. Will also perform developmental tests, such as the toxic lead poisoning check, and provide information about oral health. There are income guidelines for this program. **Source: www.fns.usda.gov/wic**

Many fast food restaurants employ teens as young as fourteen or fifteen years of age, but they must abide by Child Labor Laws. The Fair Labor Standards Act (FLSA), which prescribes standards for the basic minimum wage and overtime pay, affects most private and public employment. It requires employers to pay covered employees (who are not otherwise exempt) at least the federal minimum wage and overtime pay of one-and-one-half times the regular rate of pay. For nonagricultural operations, it restricts the hours that children under age sixteen can work and forbids the employment of children under age eighteen in certain jobs deemed too dangerous. For agricultural operations, it prohibits the employment of children under age sixteen during school hours and in certain jobs deemed too dangerous. The Act is administered by the Employment Standards Administration's Wage and Hour Division within the US Department of Labor (United States Department of Labor, 2011).

With the restrictions of these laws, you cannot work too many hours. Your paycheck will be small, and any overtime will usually be off limits.

Many individuals are resorting to online resources for earning extra money (some of these resources will be mentioned later in this book), but many of these websites require one to be either sixteen or eighteen years of age, and most of them do require a form of identification.

The best option for a new parent fifteen years of age or younger is to remain in school. I know this may sound a bit cliché, but it is true. Staying in school at this age is crucial because it is the only way to grasp important subjects that cannot be taught at home while watching television. Some of these subjects include but are not limited to having a firm understanding of math, which allows you to manage your money effectively once you are old enough to work.

School provides other non-academic benefits as well. For starters, consistent interaction among peers is priceless. Effective communication skills are essential throughout life. Talking to people within one's own age group is a reminder of youth, and it keeps a young mother from rushing into the adult years despite the "adult action" that were brought on by becoming a young mother.

Nevertheless, communication skills at this age will prepare a single mother to talk successfully with doctors, counselors, or anyone who may play an important role in the mother's and her baby's life.

Science is crucial. When I was younger, I took this subject for granted. However, when I started learning how to cook, I appreciated it more after the microwave caught on fire when I kept the aluminum foil wrapped around my fish sandwich, or after I touched a light bulb with wet hands. Many small procedures in the kitchen are based on an understanding of science. Learning about science at school prevents accidents and gives insight into how nature works in general.

If you're a teenage mother, you may ask yourself, *"Who will care for my baby while I am still in school"?* This may be a difficult question to ask if there isn't a good relationship in place with your parents. Do you have a family member with stability who knows your situation in its entirety and may be able to help you? Is there a civil, communicative relationship in place with your child's father family? Is there someone you personally know and trust who has experience with young children and has extra time throughout the day? If you were able to answer yes to any of these questions, then that gives you a good idea of who to sit down and talk with about helping you take care of your baby while you are finishing the crucial years of school.

But if you were not able to answer yes to any of these questions, it would be best to speak to a guidance counselor or other administrator who can lead you in the right direction to help care for your baby since every situation is unique or different. Then again, if you are enrolled in any of the programs mentioned above, your local county office will usually provide a voucher for a childcare facility of your choice.

If you are sixteen years of age or older, here is an overview of programs which will help any mother get started on the right track which some programs may provide daycare assistance. Each program may vary by state; so check your local listings:

Job Readiness

- **Job Corps:** This program is for those young adults in low-income groups aged sixteen to twenty-four years of age. Job Corps provides hands-on training in more than one hundred professional specialized areas, including automobile and machine repair, finance, such as accounting, and business services, medical care, IT technology, and many more trades. Job Corps also helps program participants to generate a diploma or a GED. Job Corps can help individuals who have a diploma get ready for college by establishing relationships with local institutions. Programs in independent living, employability, and social abilities are provided to all Job Corps participants in order to prepare them for a career and preparation for real life. This program is available in many states. **Source: jobcorps.gov**

PURCHASING A CAR:

- **Ways to Work:** Ways to Work is a charitable, economical loan program that helps working family members move beyond hardship by giving them access to economics and finance and efficient transportation. Ways to Work provides loans up to $6,000 for low-income families. **Source: waystowork.org**
- **Free Charity Cars:** This program gives out generously donated vehicles to those in need. You make a profile on the website and tell why you need an automobile. Next, you must produce ballots for people who will vouch for you and to verify the reasons you previously stated why you need an automobile. These ballots could be from close relatives and friends. Whoever wins the most ballots receives a car. **Source: freecharitycars.org**

CELLULAR PHONE:

- **Safe Link Wireless:** This program provides a free, no contract cell phone to income eligible households. Cell phone minutes are renewed at two hundred fifty minutes each month with this service. Only one cell phone per household. **Source: safelinkwireless.com**

NEED A HOUSE?

- **Habitat for Humanity:** Are you sick and exhausted with renting? Did you know a key to gaining success is to become a homeowner? Habitat for Humanity's home ownership system helps income-qualified individuals become homeowners by having them assist in the construction of another individual's house. Once they helped in this construction for someone else; then construction will be created for their own home. Other specifications that help a family qualify for a home through Habitat for Humanity are overcrowding and homelessness. **Source: habitat.org**
- **CoAbode:** This is a service in which single mothers help other single mothers by sharing housing. This is a matching service that connects you with other single mothers to combine financial resources, utilities, or living space. Create a profile on this website and be connected with other women who are in search of a roommate. **Source: coabode.org**

CHECK YOUR CREDIT REPORT:

- **Annual Credit Report:** Need to see your credit report? The credit report, when it is excellent allows you to have the finer things in life such as a new car, house, personal loans, etc. This service allows you to see your credit report free once a year. **Source: annualcreditreport.com**
- **Credit Karma:** On this website, you are able to see your credit rating for an endless number of times, sign up for credit rating signals when changes are made to your credit rating. This company provides its services at no cost. This site also provides benefits and education on how to increase your credit score. Note: The higher your credit rating, the more you will be able to purchase a new car, obtain a credit card with an excellent borrowing limit, and obtain other credit-based items.

Source: creditkarma.com

- **Lexington Law:** Let's say after you've reviewed your credit report and credit score and unsatisfied with items on there; this service will remove any negative items off your credit report to boost your credit score. Although, this company charges a small monthly fee, it would be worth it by the third or fourth month.

Source: lexingtonlaw.com

DISABILITY ASSISTANCE

- **Social Security Disability Insurance:** Are you disabled? Do you have an impairment, mental or physical, which may prevent you from working? Do you have proof or documentation of this impairment? If yes, you may be eligible to receive SSI or SSDI, or both. Also, do you know if you had impairment before the age of twenty-two, you could receive benefits off of your parent's record as well? Important: When applying for these benefits, it is wise to have a social security advocate or lawyer become your representative. Social Security lawyers, by law, cannot ask for money upfront. Their money comes only when you, as the disabled person, win the disability case. Some cases take longer than others, depending on the circumstances. To get started on a disability application, go to: **socialsecurity.gov**

IF YOU ARE A VETERAN'S DEPENDANT:

- **Veterans' Assistance:** If you are a dependant of a veteran or an active duty military person, then your local Veteran's Administration office can provide one-time assistance for things such as car repair, food, utility assistance, or help with paying a credit card bill. This assistance is usually available for a veteran's dependant if the caretaker has very little money to support the dependant at the end of the month. For instance, if $600.00 a month is made and

$550.00 of it went toward bills, an unexpected expense or emergency came up, such as the primary family car broke down, or your household ran out of food, then the local Veteran's Administration office can be a great resource. Again, this sort of help is available on a one-time basis for veterans and their dependants only. **Source: Contact your local Veterans' Administration office.**

MISCELLANEOUS SERVICES

- **Modest Needs:** Offers grant assistance to individuals who may need help with paying a bill. You must fill out an application on their website. **Source: Modestneeds.org**

Health Services

This section consists of a few programs that offer assistance due to health- related reasons. Keep in mind that whether you are working, attending school, or simply still trying to find your way in the world, your health, and the consistent maintenance of it, should always be your first priority.

You're going to get sick eventually, and when it happens, why not be prepared for it? Purchasing prescription medications can be very costly, but programs such as YourRxCard and The Free Drug Card Program help significantly with these costs. If you do not have health insurance, or are not eligible to receive government-funded health insurance such as Medicaid, then refer to these:

- **Ameriplan:** This plan provides a discount and charges a small fee for services such as chiropractors, dentistry, general health, vision, prescriptions, and urgent care.

Source: ameriplanusa.com
- **Health Well Foundation:** This program provides medical assistance to individuals with certain diseases or medical conditions. See their website for criteria.

Source: healthwellfoundation.org
- **Patient Services Incorporated:** This program provides medical assistance to individuals with certain diseases or medical conditions. See their website for certain criteria.

Source: patientservicesinc.org

OTHER SERVICES

In order to use some of the information in this book successfully, you will need some computer skills, Internet access, and a computer. But these are not necessary just for this book; having some internet skills and a computer with access to the internet in the home is extremely important for successful living in the twenty-first century. We live in an informational based society, and more employers and resources in general are posting their services online. If you do not have a computer or access to the internet (such as at the public library), a company called Internet Essentials offers free training on using the Internet, a computer for less than $150.00, and Internet service for ten dollars a month. The requirement of this wonderful service is that you must be a Comcast member for ninety days and have a child eligible for the reduced price lunch at school.

Source: internetessentials.com

Please remember that there are hundreds of services out there, but the particular ones mentioned in this chapter are sure to be helpful when you are starting out as a mother, or you just basically need help.

The next chapter will focus on the most common financial resources promoted for single mothers. However, what concerns me about these resources is that they are designed to keep you penny pinching with just enough to get by from month to month. Chapter 2 will discuss methods to stretch your money as far as possible. Any method I discuss that you are successful with and make money with, keep in mind that you must report this income to your local county office if you are receiving county benefits or any other form of federal assistance.

CHAPTER 2

Types of Income (Most) Single Mothers Are Exposed to, and Ten Ways to Flip Them

Staying in constant motion leads to stable progress.
- Anonymous

Before I attended college, I used to wonder why college was so important. Now I understand — the government will literally pay you to read a book. Of course, money isn't everything, but it helps. Everywhere I turned on the Internet, even on the television, there was some advertisement about going back to school. It's a great thing because it doesn't matter whether you are a freshman, sophomore, junior, senior, a graduate student, or earning your doctorate, you can receive money to attend college. And the higher the college level, the more money you will receive.

When I was in graduate school, I would receive a check from $5,000- $8,500 each term, and a term lasted about ten to twelve weeks, or three months. This meant that twice a year, I would receive this check. And boy was I happy to receive this extra money — it tremendously came in handy. Every school, whether it is a trade school or university, has its own particular payout system with the refund process, so it is important to ask about financial aid when applying for admissions. The school administrative staff usually will not volunteer this type of information because they want the student focused on academics and not just the money. On another note, some schools do not issue refunds at all. These schools just use the excess federal aid to cover books and miscellaneous school expenses. So again, it is important to ask questions about financial aid and a disbursement check during the admissions process.

This is often the first form of income single mothers are exposed to: **the financial aid refund check**. To start receiving a refund check, you must have a GED or high school diploma. Certain community colleges will allow you to take a test to determine if you qualify for admission. In the state of Ohio, it's called the ability to benefit test. If you don't have a diploma and you pass the test, you can still receive federal aid and take classes, but I don't recommend this, especially if you want to transfer to a university after you earn your associate's degree at the community college.

If you do have a diploma, I would recommend choosing three schools you may be interested in attending. Fill out the admissions application for each school and pay the application fee, keep in mind that some fees can be waived, depending on your circumstances. Then, the waiting process begins.

Once you have a response, the school administration will require more information from you, such as a letter of recommendation and high school or college transcripts. The next step is to fill out the FAFSA. Be certain to get the school code from the school you want to attend. The official FAFSA website is fafsa.ed.gov. Any other website asking you to pay, even a small ninety-nine cent fee, is a scam. During the FAFSA application process, you will need a PIN, which you create while on the website. Once the FAFSA is completed, your information will automatically be sent to the school(s) you listed on the application. Next, you will receive a SAR (Student Aid Report), which summarizes all the information you listed on the FAFSA. Make sure the information is accurate because this information is sent to the school you may want to attend for the next two to six years of your life. Once you've looked over the information and verified that it is correct, look at the Expected Family Contribution (EFC) code. Let's assume the EFC is a zero. This means you can receive the maximum in federal aid, grants, loans, scholarships, and work-study programs.

The school(s) you listed on the FAFSA will contact you once they receive your information. At this point, they will send one of these three: **1) a financial aid award letter, 2) a letter stating they need more information from you to verify your financial need, 3) or a letter stating that you are not eligible for financial aid.** To prevent these last two, make sure there you don't have any previous defaulted student loans and that the information on your FAFSA is correct.

The next type of income (s) I want to touch <u>briefly</u> on is that which you can earn from a home-based business. These include starting a typing service, drop shipping, and operating a mobile hair care service, among hundreds of other business ideas. A good book I recommend is *Mind Your Own Business: The Best Businesses You Can Start Today for Under $500* by Stephen Wagner. Although this book came out in 1992, it is still an awesome book to get the creative juices flowing. Whenever I want to try a new hobby or make extra money for the holidays, I use an idea or two from this reference book.

Another income that most people are exposed to is employment, or non-taxable income such as county benefits, but any further mention of this is speaking the obvious. But even if you have a steady source of employment, can you honestly live off forty hours a week at a 9:00 a.m. to 5:00 p.m. job? If you get sick and can't work, it would be ideal to have more than enough money for bills. Wouldn't you like to have enough money to put in savings, too? I understand — the feeling can be overwhelming if you do not know how to accomplish this. Or, perhaps you are looking for a job and thus need extra money now. Job-hunting in itself can cause a financial and emotional strain on a single mother. Think of it this way: you will have to buy some professional outfits and have gas money to get to and from interviews. What if the company keeps calling you back for several interviews, but in the end, you still don't get the job? If you *do* get the job, you'll need money to get to work every day, and you won't be paid for another two to three weeks. It is tough to keep going in circles like this, and with today's unemployment rates, <u>it is</u> <u>a circle</u>.

It is time for a back-up plan that puts you in a better financial position than you were yesterday. Here are five ways to flip your income online and offline: **Note: These ways are not listed in any particular order; please choose whichever suits you the best.**

1. **Affiliate marketing (promoting other companies products)** - Affiliate marketing may sound like a complex master income generating method. Actually, it's one of the easiest methods for generating an income online, and it's not complicated to understand or to put into practice. Affiliate marketing moved from the traditional markets to the internet market, and when it did, it found a new identity. It is an easy yet powerful way to earn cash on the internet, in which the affiliate, which is you, can earn a commission in return for generating sales/leads from promoting various company products on your website.

Using affiliate marketing, the seller grows her/his chances of success by reaching a greater audience through the efforts of the company, and the companies earn cash by selling a market ready product without having to take any risk by investing any of her/his own cash. While it takes some general knowledge and effort to be an Internet success in this sort of marketing, the one thing that sets affiliate marketing apart from other online internet income-generating opportunities is that it doesn't require any special skills or years of training to begin earning money.

Just like any new job, trade, or skill, as a newcomer to working on the internet, you will face many challenges, but if you follow these three easy steps, you are almost certain to succeed:

Step 1: What types of things are you interested in? The first step is to discover a market that fascinates you or something that you are enthusiastic about. Like any other job, doing what you appreciate is an important aspect in attaining achievement in this income plan. You can use any search engine or online forum to discover what people are purchasing or talking about. Perhaps you can do an online search using the keywords **the top ten purchases of 2012**. Choose a particular market to focus on and keep with it. Going from market to market will not get you far in affiliate marketing. **Remember: stick with one product.** An example of a hot and successful market would be the weight-loss market.

Step 2: Now that you know what type of industry you are going to promote, it is essential to find a high earning, quick payout, and useful product to promote. This can be done by going to Internet marketplaces for affiliates such as ClickBank and Commission Junction. Signing up with these websites is free, and they can be used to research products pertaining to the niche you are interested in. ClickBank is easier to sign up for since after you make an account, you click on a category and choose the best product for you; once you've done that, you will be given a "hop link" or a website URL to promote. Commission Junction's process is similar, but some products need approval before they can be promoted. Upon being approved, you will be given a unique web link. Whenever someone uses this web link or hop link to go to the retailer's purchase web page and that person buys the product, you will be compensated in the form of a commission, which can range from a few dollars to several hundred dollars depending on the type of product you choose. Keep in mind that using more than one internet marketing technique increases your chances of earning a regular income. **Source: clickbank.com and comissionjunction.com**

Step 3: This is the most important step for earning cash with online affiliate marketing. Now that you have chosen your market and the item you want to promote, you need to market the item. This can and should be done often—at least once a week or once a month. You can create a website or a weblog, and soon you will start getting online visitors. You can also use your website to write reviews of products and content pertaining to an item. Both these methods are powerful ways of advertising an item through your site/blog.

Content is another great way to market goods and services. Content includes writing articles, and this can drive traffic to your page since the Internet is a place where millions of people turn to for information. Once your page gets visitors who use your links, you will earn money, but first, you need to get the word out about your website. I personally recommend using a site called **Fiverr.com**. People will promote the product you choose, write one or more articles, and drive traffic to your website, or do any other type of Internet marketing or Search Engine Optimization (SEO) for five dollars!

Imagine using ten different services on this website to promote your product for exactly fifty dollars a month. This is an amazing deal compared to the companies that charge more than a thousand dollars a month for something a worker on Fiverr. com will do for five dollars.

Another way to promote your affiliate links is to use websites such as Yahoo answers and ehow.com to answer questions people ask online or to create how-to guides relevant to your market. Considering how many individuals use these websites every day, it is the easiest and quickest way to market an item. In fact, this is the number one way seasoned entrepreneurs generate income because it's a targeted market. Since you are answering questions relevant to your market, the individuals asking the questions are most likely already looking for such an item. Plus, there is no cost to you since you do not have to buy your own website. Also, since these websites are already getting a lot of daily visitors, you do not have to worry about getting visitors to your own site. Instead, you can focus all of your efforts on writing good content that will lead individuals to buy the items you're advertising. This method is also good for building links, and links are vital for any website or blog to get off the ground.

Having links to your website is the life of traffic-short and long term traffic. To gain a full understanding of link building, I recommend reading *How to Backlink: Using the New Linkerati to Reach Page 1 of Google* by Brian Horn.

Online promotion requires a lot of determination, but if you are persistent and motivated, the rewards can be great. After all, affiliate promotion was one of the earliest and best ways to generate income online.

Recommended reading:

- *Mind Your Own Business: The Best Businesses You Can Start Today for Under $500* by Stephen Wagner.
- *How to Backlink: Using the New Linkerati To Reach Page 1 of Google* by Brian Horn

The Gerber Life College Plan: Earlier in this book, I touched briefly on my childhood, and one aspect of it was the death of my father. I am pretty certain at the time he thought he would be around forever, or that he was invincible. Many individuals in general believe they will live forever, but to think this way is "selfish", especially when you are a parent. Death is a sensitive, sad, but normal process of life. As a parent, you always have to be somewhat ready for your time to depart, and to live your life in a way that makes your children comfortable when the time comes. This is why the Gerber Life College Plan is an excellent resource to provide both. It works like a savings fund, college plan, and life insurance all in one, unlike term life insurance policies that only cover funeral expenses or other bills after someone dies. Many insurance policies also build cash value over time, but they do not accrue very quickly, and a larger amount of the insurance is usually not available until the third or fourth year (or longer). Even in some scenarios, you would be lucky to have five hundred dollars of cash value in the policy by the end of the fourth year. This is what makes the Gerber Life College Plan so great and different from other insurances. It works like this:

Let's say you decide to choose an amount of $25,000 for a college plan. Depending on the age of the child, you would pay on average of around $142 a month. If you are enrolled in school and receiving financial aid refunds, or you are following the other "flip it" methods of earning income discussed in this chapter, I recommend that you pay the premiums every six months or once a year. In this way, you can forget that the policy is in place altogether until you really need it. The cool thing about the Gerber Life College Plan is that you are not allowed to access any cash until after the first year, in which you will have close to fifteen hundred dollars available after the first year. As each year passes and the money is left untouched, the amount of money available to you grows higher. Let's say you chose a ten-year, $25,000

college plan. Gerber will send you a check for twenty-five thousand dollars at the end of the ten-year period. In the event that you pass away before the ten-year period ends, Gerber will automatically send the full $25,000 check to the beneficiary of your plan, unlike many other insurance policies that only pay out what has been paid in. **Source: gerberlife.com**

Selling Online Domains: An online domain is just as important as having a residence address, only it is more important in the world of the Internet. Website addresses such as walmart. com or shoes.com (among millions of others) are domains. Some domains are worth a few dollars, and some are worth several hundred thousand dollars. To get started with buying and selling domains online, all you need is five to ten dollars to purchase a domain. There are many websites where you can purchase a domain without spending much money: **register. com** and **namecheap.com** are a few. I personally recommend **godaddy.com** for the many benefits and discounts it offers when buying a domain.

However, do your research about selling domains online. The best place to begin this research is **Namepros.com**. Next, it is important to narrow down which particular category or niche you want to focus on with selling domains. Once you know exactly what type of niche you will be working with, you can utilize several free tools:

- **Stuckdomains.com** — Type in a keyword and it will bring up old or expired domains. These domains are available for sale.
- **Estibot.com** — This site offers five free domain appraisals per day; services start at $29.95 a month for any more domains that need appraising.
- **Google Search Keyword Tool** — Type a keyword into the Google search engine. The greater the number of people searching for the term, the more a domain with those particular search terms may be worth.

After following these steps, you should be ready to sell the domains you have chosen. Some of the best places to sell domains are on **Sedo.com**, **Flippa.com**, **ebay.com**, and **forums.digitalpoint.com**.

Freelancing: Increasingly popular sites like **elance.com**, **Guru. com**, **Odesk.com**, or **Freelancer.com** are becoming a common way to make money online. One year I made close to $6,000 on Elance. com. If you can write an article, type a form or letter, research a topic such as the "healthiest foods to eat in America", then you can succeed with freelancing. These sites offer introductory memberships so that you can get a feel for how they work, but regular memberships will run you around ten dollars or more a month. This membership cost is definitely worth every dime.

Drop Shipping: Drop shipping is considered one of the most profitable online businesses of the twenty-first century. Drop shipping works like this: let's say you are interested in selling computers on the Internet. The first step is to find a reliable, trustworthy drop shipping company rated good or excellent by the BBB and whose specialty is electronics. Research the company before you sign up. Some companies charge a small membership fee; others don't. An amazing drop shipper I recommend is **dropshipaccess.com**. This company charges a one-time fee of $295.00 or $695.00 depending on the services you choose. When you sign up with dropshipaccess.com, they will provide you with your own online store, which is important since you will be drop shipping.

Once you have signed up and chosen which products you want to sell, you will need to create a seller's account with **ebay. com** and **Amazon.com**. When you've done that, you will list the products you are selling along with photos and descriptions of the products. Of course, you will set the prices of the products higher than what you pay for them so that a <u>profit</u> can be made. It's a great idea to create an online store on Amazon.com, as that is the number one marketplace to sell anything. Millions of online consumers will choose Amazon over Wal-Mart any day, and Amazon.com will bring customers and great traffic without much effort.

Let's say you've listed around ten different types of computers/products to become familiar with drop shipping and you've received your first order. You will then turn around and immediately order the product from your drop-shipper. But with drop shipping, you will never be required to hold any inventory because the drop shipper ships the product to the customer on your behalf. The only important tasks required are placing orders, providing tracking numbers to the customers, and collecting profits. Keep in mind that Amazon.com and Ebay.com has extremely strict rules when it comes to selling products, but if you know and learn the rules of the game and you work within those rules, you will make money.

CHAPTER 3

Five Ways to Relieve Stress

During these periods of relaxation after concentrated intellectual activity, the intuitive mind seems to take over and can produce the sudden clarifying insights, which give so much joy and delight.
- Fritjof Capra

After reading chapters one and two, it's time to take a break from all of the hard thinking. The strategies and tips provided in the previous chapters can be satisfying, especially when you have applied them correctly and you are seeing the results of increased income. However, there must be a balance in life between raising children, and being the primary breadwinner. As a single parent, it is important to relax your mind, body, and soul. This is why this entire chapter is focused on just that — **relaxation**.

As a mother, you owe it to yourself to be able to calm your mind from the hectic duties of day-to-day life. Relaxation involves more than watching television, drinking coffee, or just taking time to be lazy. One way to do this is to use creative thinking, which allow us to instantly take notice of our thoughts, emotions, and memories without immediately categorizing them as good or bad. We have to be more thoughtful toward ourselves, address our thoughts, and use our own thoughts as a companion, rather than letting them confuse or dominate us. In doing this, we become better able to control how we want to act in challenging circumstances. Creative thinking also allows us to be more conscious of the present. By being one with our thoughts, we can become less terrified and confused by them, and thus less inspired to evade them with harmful routines or activities that do not bring inner peace.

We can also understand plenty about ourselves, particularly all the societal demands we have internalized, such as our views on how much we weigh... If creative thinking does not appeal to you; try maintaining a journal of key activities throughout your day, and what you think about your experiences within them. Something in particular may activate your secret yearnings or thoughts, such as to tame a challenging connection with another person, go to a restaurant where you really want to eat but choosing not to, or just taking a risk like sky-diving, etc. Write down what is going on in your life, and then think about what you're going through. It is likely that you will identify a connection between your most difficult situations and stressors. Use your analytical capabilities to consider why those particular stressors are causing any sort of negative thoughts in your mind.

Once you have identified them, close your eyes in a quiet atmosphere, and envision a positive image of yourself. In this visual picture, observe this positive you going about your usual daily activities, and pretend this is another person altogether. What are the relationships with her family like? Are they positive and happy? Or negative and unhappy? What does she do to relax after a stressful day? Does she have the same job you have? Does she like that job? What are her connections with other people? Are they the same connections you currently have? How does she feel about those connections?

Now return to the actual you and reflect on how these thoughts make you feel. Is there a sensation of pleasure as you consider the possibilities of the positive you? Or is there disappointment and defeat? Focus on what exactly is going through your thoughts. You are likely to discover harmful ideas that you have internalized because of society's information about what you (and all females) should be.

Next, visualize your more positive self again while saying to yourself, "*I will be gentle with myself*". "*I will take care of who I am*". "*I will be genuine*". After saying this to yourself, does the positive you look different this time? Are there aspects about her that now look more like the actual you? Which features of her lifestyle are similar to your actual lifestyle? For example, perhaps the new positive you has quite a different connection with her partner than you do. Or perhaps she has a pleasant evening without liquor, when the actual you needs to consume an alcoholic beverage to relax. Does she have interest in, and feel empowered by, her work while the actual you is always exhausted and unmotivated?

The goal here is seeking change in each routine or methods of living that you want to shift toward, rather than aspects of your life that you want to prevent or give up. You must be willing to set in motion these positive objectives. Compose a record of simple, daily activities that you find pleasant, and that are relatively simple to do. These actions can raise your positive feelings, and help you to stop worrying about or over thinking your life. Do as much as you can to shift yourself towards a more improved personal character without determining whether if it is good or bad. This exercise will help you prepare for this within the chapter.

In addition, this chapter focuses on some of the more creative ways to relax. From using turmeric powder to enjoying your body with a dildo, these five creative ways of relaxing will wind down your day.

1. **Turmeric Powder:** Turmeric root extract has grown in India for centuries. Next, Chinese suppliers in 700 AD, Eastern African-Americans by 800 AD, and Western African-Americans by 1200 AD distributed it. Then, it was presented somewhere in the Barbados in the eighteenth century. Today, turmeric powder is widely developed

and used throughout the tropics. Turmeric powder's main extract is said to be one of nature's most highly effective healers. This powder has a variety of uses from treating small cuts to enjoying a luxurious bubble bath. Turmeric powder does it all.

Here are some of the benefits of turmeric powder:

Antiseptic: The main extract is known for its germ-killing features and it is very beneficial as a disinfectant. Actually, there are a lot of germ-killing lotions that use turmeric as their primary ingredient.

Detoxifier: Turmeric powder's main extract is also known for its cleansing capabilities. It is said to be the best organic detoxifier for the liver, and its use is suggested in cases where a person may be vulnerable to liver damage. For proper use, drink two tablespoons of pure turmeric juice a day.

Anti-Depressant: This charming yellow-colored powder has been used efficiently by ancient cultures such as the Chinese and the Indians to treat depressive disorders. Today it is still used for this purpose.

To avoid the development of tumors: Turmeric powder's main extract suppresses the development of tumors in the body. Those individuals who suffer from cancer are recommended in some cases to take turmeric powder in a tablet form.

Weight Loss: Since turmeric has features that help the metabolic rate, it helps to suppress weight gain. Those looking to support their exercise plans should add turmeric to their diet. A small bit of turmeric adds both taste and weight-loss features to vegetables.

Other important uses of turmeric powder, which may not necessarily be used for stress, are as follows:

- Turmeric powder is associated with fertility and success, and brings good luck wherever it is being used.
- Turmeric powder can be added to creams and bath water to enhance the natural glow of the skin or create a golden glow. Millions of women of the Indian culture use it for this purpose. **Source: turmeric.com**

2. **Dildos:** This stress relief method is intended for the mature reader only. I chose this as a stress relief method because a dildo eliminates stress and it calms the nerves. It also can assist in making better personal health decisions. Since a dildo is on the topic of sex, it is important to mention that sex can be a wonderful, beautiful situation when it is done with someone who has mutual feelings for you. But sex can also be a breeding ground for bad decisions as well. These decisions can include: calling someone for drunken sex, a regretful one-night stand, which could be a crazy stranger or a lunatic, sexually transmitted diseases (especially the ones that won't go away with creams or pills), heartache, obsession, and unwanted pregnancy. A dildo is an accessible sexual toy that can be used to soothe tension and stress. It comes in all sizes and forms. If you are a single mother, in some cases, it may be difficult to discern lust from love for the man you had a child with, especially if it is not a good or healthy situation. Furthermore, you don't want to have another child out of wedlock, if it is not by choice. Keep in mind that a dildo should not replace the total affection you can receive from another human being, but it definitely assists in staying focused, and most importantly, it is a terrific stress reliever. There is absolutely no reason to be ashamed of using one.

3. **Music Therapy at Home:** This stress-relief method is used by a large number of therapists in their professional

practices, but it can also be used at home. Music therapy can be a calming process; one uses songs in a focused way to help improve one's overall well-being. The exciting thing about music therapy is that you can do it with your children. It may seem like a game at first, but music actually activates very important elements within the brain. To practice music therapy with your children, think of a song you and your kids are familiar with, and allow them to be creative by making homemade instruments from items found around the home. Just allow yourself to be free and have fun!

4. **Beginner Mediation:** To begin mediation, set aside a certain time every day, preferably early in the morning before the day's events take place. Slowing your respiration decreases your pulse rate, calms the muscle tissue, concentrates the mind, and is an ideal way to begin this exercise. Concentrate on the way you breathe. Before beginning any sort of exercise or extraneous movement of the body, you need to stretch. Extending your body releases the muscle tissue, enabling you to sit or lie down better. Beginners must realize that mediation is an active procedure. The art of concentrating and letting go is an effort, and you have to be intentionally engaged! It is very typical for someone new to mediation to have thoughts such as, *"Hey, what am I doing here"*? or *"Why can't I just quiet my rattling thoughts already"*? When this happens, concentrate on your breathing and let the disappointment go. Those who are beginners at meditation should observe their bodies when the trance-like state begins. Once the mind quiets, focus on your toes and then gradually shift your way up through your body (including your inner organs). This is very healthy and an indication that you are on the right track.

5. **Give and Receive Joy:** One year, around the Christmas holiday, I cleaned up a bunch of my kids' toys that were

not being played with anymore. I instructed my youngest son to pick out the toys he no longer wanted so that another child could enjoy them. I cleaned the toys, sanitized them, and took them to the local Goodwill. When you donate to charity, the organization will give you either a coupon or receipt, which can be used for tax purposes. But I honestly didn't care about receiving anything. About a week later, I was in the same Goodwill looking at some old books when I noticed that there was a child a few feet away from me who seemed excited and ecstatic about something. I looked up and saw that he was holding my son's old toy. But I wanted to be certain, so I had to get closer. I pretended as though I was looking at something in the toy section, and yes; it was his toy. What my son had wanted to throw in the trash had brightened another child's day. The point is, no matter your religious or personal beliefs, it is important to "plant good seeds" in life because no matter what you do, it always comes back.

After realizing that I had given unselfishly, I had wonderful things happen to me out of the ordinary. Unexpected amounts of money came my way, and people that I hadn't spoken to in years suddenly phoned me. I gained new friendships and more peace within my mind and heart. Giving to others became a monthly ritual for my children and me, even if we donated just one item we were no longer using in the household. These items can be clothes, silverware, toys, or home décor items. Anything that is no longer being used can be donated for someone else in need. But the end result is that the gift of giving brings abundance or prosperity.

CHAPTER 4

Bringing out the Best in You and A Creative Way to make that Happen Today

Want to know the difference between a poor person and a rich person? Nothing; it's all about how you spend your twenty-four hours. - Anonymous

My mother always told me, "You don't want to be working some-one else's dream the rest of your life." If you're wondering what this means, I will break it down: That job you have or that pro-fession you're in—the one you get up and go to work for every day—is technically someone else's dream.

Some individuals may really enjoy their work and would not leave it for the world. Each person is entitled to his or her own preferences. But you are still a part of someone else's dream. You are just a small but "almost" important part of it. The reason why you are an *almost* important part of it is that you are generating sales, which equal profit for that person's dream. The person who created this dream can sleep very well at night and live comfortably, all thanks to your hard work, sweat, and tears. On the contrary, the reason why you are a small part of the dream is that you are disposable. Think of a toothbrush or a disposable razor you may use to shave your legs. Yes, you are that easy to replace, regardless of how excellent your performance is. You may be on good terms with the person (your boss) who created the dream, but that won't buy you complete financial security. Those who believe that what I am saying may not apply to them are usually the first ones to be replaced with a fresher, friendlier face.

As a single mother or parent in general carrying all the responsibilities on your shoulders, you don't want to keep going through this process throughout life, do you? When you ask yourself questions such as, *Isn't there more to life than working or getting up every day to do the same thing?* You are slowly beginning to merge on the right track. The dream will slowly begin to surface, and sometimes in unusual ways. This is when the dream will tug at you, and you won't be able to get it out of your mind.

My dream surfaced shortly after I completed my Bachelor's degree. I worked part- time in a pharmacy while waiting for responses to the resumes I had sent to various employers in my field of study. One sunny afternoon, after I had settled comfortably in my position as a pharmacy technician, my youngest son's daycare called me at my job. My son had a high fever, and he was vomiting.

I immediately left work to pick him up, and I took him to the emergency room, where they told me he had pneumonia in his left lung.

Meanwhile, as serious as the situation was, I needed to be at work or the bills would not been paid. My son's illness required me to miss a lot of time from work, and honestly, I felt that it was unfair to have to choose.

By the second week of missing days at work, I called my job and respectfully thanked the supervisor for employing me, but that "I would not be returning". Something deep inside of me wanted something else. I wanted to share my story and communicate my voice to the many women who shared common interests or experienced the same problems as me. Night after night, I worked diligently on my story into the early morning hours while my children slept. I felt passionate about every word, as if my fingers were unable to rest. I finally understood why I had been born and what my purpose is — it is to write.

However, not everyone may understand how to discover his or her dream or creative ability, or true potential, at first.

If you do not know what you want to do with your life, you are going to encounter a certain amount of emotional pain or strain with any job you have. The issue here is not the job. Keep working while you create aspirations within yourself to fulfill your dream.

How do you create an aspiration if you do not have one?
- Think back to your childhood years. What did you want to do then? Is there a spark of something left? Could it be ignited?
- Be sincere with yourself. Do you have a key desire that you are not confessing to anyone — perhaps not even to yourself? Are you humiliated to confess that what you really want to do is become an expert professional golfer or to dance on Broadway? Let the aspirations out of the closet. Even if you are without the resources to achieve it absolutely, it can be achieved in varying capacities that fit your current life.
- Make a targeted attempt to determine what might grab your attention.
- Spend as little time as possible viewing TV or playing video games.

These types of pleasures steal your time and energy and deaden your creativity.

- If you dug deeply into the absolute depths of your being and still came up with nothing, do not worry. What I found is this: Passion comes from working on or creating something you value highly. If you keep your thoughts focused on what you love, something will come.
- **Focus on creativity-the key to unlocking your true potential.**

Creativity is the process of bringing something new into existence. When you make something, you are actually bringing it into being — making it from nothing. But how do you make something from nothing? How do you accomplish creativity? What is the substance of creativity? Perhaps only a miracle can describe creativity, that rapid "aha!" moment when it all comes together. Some have said that it's something strange and confusing, perhaps difficult to determine. Some have said it must be a motivation. Creativity is simply considering the difficult, and then doing what no one has done before.

Creativity comes in many forms. It can be medical creativity, leading to new technology or new types of healthcare treatments. It can even be as simple as designs and artistry, such as a simple painting. The main thing to keep in mind is that creativity encompasses having an idea and then implementing that idea.

Children are inquisitive and extremely innovative, especially when playing. They do not yet understand that some things cannot be done. They have no innovative boundaries; no one has told them that they cannot do something. They are courageous travelers, performers, and musicians. They have not yet been compelled to adjust, and they think that they can do anything or everything. Our innovative capabilities often appear very early in life. Analysis has shown that most adults only come up with three to four different ideas for a situation, while most kids will come up with fifty creative ideas for any given situation or problem.

It is known that as far as creativity is concerned, the amount is equal to excellence. Creativity has been meticulously instilled into our nature; it is in our DNA.

Unfortunately, as we mature, the demands of having to get a job or beginning a household all seem to hold back our creativity.

The pressure of our daily existence, in addition to the periodic challenges of life, holds us back. But creativity is crucial to our well-being. Without creativity, our life immediately becomes scheduled and boring.

The next important aspect for achieving creativity is to think imaginatively in your preferred field. Perseverance is required — that determination to keep on working with an issue until it is solved. You must know when to break solutions down and look at them diversely — when to nurture the process of creativity and when to let it relax until it is willing to fly free.

Another important tool to look for in harnessing creativity is the courage to try something you've never tried before. You have to be able to embrace whatever new opportunities present themselves to you. You never know when thoughts will come. <u>You must be passionate about success regardless of setbacks.</u> It doesn't matter what the result turns out to be. Your interest in doing something is all that's important to make it work; regardless of what it is you want to do.

Most of all, you must experience any innovative risk with the mind of a child — keep your thoughts open and free of restriction. Even kids may not recognize it, but fun time is a real learning experience. It is the mind's preferable way to solve problems and understand solutions. The kinds of things that are discovered through this sort of learning process are **numbers, speaking abilities, songs, visible artistry, and culture.**

Childlike creativity should be mimicked because it is unhindered. You should believe that anything, even something extravagant, is possible. A non-creative individual says, "I can't" or "I don't know how," while an innovative individual says, "I can, and here is how." If you have the capability to see, talk, hear, or comprehend, then you are able to be innovative. Whatever you say or believe about yourself can become true. Let us return to the concept of being more childlike, unhampered by the everyday pressures of life.

How to ignite creativity (the simple way):

Pick up an illustration pad and colorful pens, and sketch groups and styles. Your kids can be a part of this activity, too. Create designs using extravagant colors, just as kids do. Color or scribble like a child. Discover the joys of Play-Doh and sculpting with clay. You don't have to make anything in particular; just have fun with it. Squish, cut, shape, and then mash the clay in all one lump again. Try creating even more forms with the clay.

You may ask yourself, "What in the world is the purpose of all this nonsense?" Well, there is no purpose; you just need to have fun, and be free. It is astonishing how much your brain will appreciate this purposeless fun time. You will instantly discover that you are more comfortable. Even your breathing is different while you're enjoying yourself. Instead of the brief, superficial breathing you do when you're feeling burdened or stressed, you're now breathing deeply. You're not suffering from the "fight or flight" feeling, but instead you're feeling completely comfortable.

Just a few moments a day of "no purpose" play will create a globe of distinction in your creative ability, troubleshooting skills, meditating, training for a skill or anything else you do. You will soon recognize it's time to take that ability to the next stage, so let that creativity come out more often and let yourself go.

Keep in mind, though, that ability is not enough. You must have overall interest and self-discipline to grow your creativity. You must be devoted to sharpening your ability.

The creativity you have within must go somewhere or be used for something, or you will soon feel disappointed and unsatisfied without knowing exactly why. The following are some of the advantages of including creativity in your daily routine:

- Self-confidence
- Reduced stress
- Inner peace
- Better management of your life
- Unbelievable fulfillment (expressing yourself or discovering your purpose)

By implementing creativity in all aspects of your lifestyle, you will discover even more advantages.

So, how do you apply your creative power to your everyday life? Begin with one specified area. You must apply those outstanding new thoughts with a perspective. Enabling your creativity demonstrates that you can be aggressive in whatever it is you want to accomplish. You can look at something that everyone else has dismissed as unimportant, but you will see it in a different light. Give it that fresh perspective. Go with the expectation of your instincts, and with the unique understanding that you as an innovative individual have to offer.

Now that you are an innovative individual, and you are more innovative than you ever imagined you could be, it's time to put that ability to test and exercise it.

The very first factor you need is a place in which to be creative — one that is relaxed and free of diversion and disturbance. Turn on some music to build the mood of the room. Pick up a pen/pencil and piece of paper. Be certain to write every idea that comes to mind, no matter how foolish or unusual it might seem.

Be aware that there are opponents to creativity. Anything that prevents the organic circulation of creativity is an opponent that tries to prevent you from being creative. There are also several opponents to your innovative time. These arise to prevent your innovative concepts from developing. Although they may seem complicated, you can deflect them.

Sometimes, the activities of everyday life can steal the innovative time necessary for creativity, such as looking after your kids and other daily pressures of living. First, make creativity a priority over your everyday lifestyle. Begin with just a few moments to yourself. Use your journal to record the problems you face and exercise a plan to come up with some innovative ways to work through them.

The worst opponent to creativity is trying to pay attention to more than one task at a time, or trying to have conscious awareness and subconscious attention simultaneously. If your lifestyle is traumatic, that just means you need creative time more than ever. You need this personal time for your inspiration, or you'll have nothing to give to others in your own life.

If you come home from a lengthy day of work, and then you have children challenging your time or energy, it is ideal to utilize the creativity discussed throughout this chapter. By using your creativity with your kids, you are assisting them to develop their self-esteem and self-confidence. Besides, kids really like having fun with their parents. As a mother, compliment them generously to help increase their own creativity and sense of self-worth.

After your children are in bed, it is important to have a few moments to sit silently and think about your own ideas. Relaxation is a fantastic way to calm your thoughts so that you can concentrate on creativity. When you refer back to your journal, you may be pleased at how efficiently you have fixed any issues you have confronted. Making meditation an aspect of your day could make all the difference in your feelings and in your overall wellness.

Another possibility for putting your creativity to the task, as with any issue throughout your life, you must first determine its underlying reason. You cannot find success in a particular goal without understanding exactly what it is you want. Once you have figured out the objective, it is time to attain that objective. What do you need to get from A to B? You need a strategy. Here is where your creativity can help you again. Create your strategy, write down how to get what you want, step by step, and finish with an agenda, if necessary. Then adhere to your agenda.

You must have a plan, an objective to accomplish, or a map of where you want to go in your life. When we have clearly described objectives, we become devoted to completing the everyday tasks necessary for achieving those objectives.

Without a certain objective regarding your life and your creative expression (s), you might discover yourself going along with another person's goals that aren't right for you as stated earlier in this chapter by "living someone else's dream". Go with your own creativity and discover what is right to suit your needs.

Obstacles of creativity:

You may experience a deficiency of self-confidence or ongoing worry. To get over this, you must continually and regularly tell yourself that you are a creative individual. Take actions to understand what you need to know in order to create whatever you want to accomplish. The key here is not to let anyone or anything deter you. There will always be someone or something better, and you must understand the art of "neglecting negativity".

You may even be a bit self-critical concerning your own capabilities. That inner voice is the toughest of them all; because that is the primary voice you listen to most of the time. This is that small voice in your ear that says, *"What do you think you can come up with to this problem that someone hasn't thought of or done already?"* or *"Who do you think you are, anyway?"* It requires some determination to change your inner voice while you are in the center of developing your creativity, but it is essential that you change the tune of your inner voice to your advantage.

One of the toughest challenges to creativity is procrastination. That innovative endeavor that shows signs of an amazing idea, that piece of creativity that is constantly on the verge of your thoughts, reaching out to you — it is so near, you can almost feel it, but it stubbornly remains out of your reach and is constantly there to taunt you, mainly because you are "stalling". Procrastination prevents progress more than any other factor because it seems like a legitimate reason, but it is not.

There are many kinds of procrastinators. There are those who delay until the last moment and tell themselves that they perform better under stress. However, stress or no stress, they still do not achieve anything. There are those who either worry about failing or worry about the outcome of the achievement, so they stall and prevent the completion of the project. Also, there are those who are not determined, deciding that if they make no choice, they are not responsible for the outcome.

The last obstacle of creativity is to cope with perfectionism. The perfectionist is an individual who never fulfilled with what he or she accomplishes. It is never quite right, it's not "perfect," or others may not like it. For example, many new authors encounter this issue. They write a few books or stories, and then they change the manuscript repeatedly, thinking it is simpler to do that than just waiting patiently until the publication process is complete. The issue with that concept is that you will never get further than those first few pages.

Many individuals get so trapped in the rut of perfection that they gradually quit the project or idea completely. If they can't get it just right, why hassle with completing it? This is very dangerous to the creative process. Perfection does not exist; therefore, demanding it of yourself is ineffective and a waste of creative time. There are societies of artists all over the globe who tell themselves of their own worth by intentionally going along with a defect in their art. The Japanese call it a wabi. This hearkens back to childlike creativity. Kids don't care if they get something ideal or perfect; they just really like doing it. They just keep on trying; regardless of how many time they fall short to accomplish perfection. Keep in mind the time when you were a kid and did not accomplish something for anyone but yourself. "Just do your best," your mother informed you. "All you can do is your best." As life moves along, certain changes occur that are beyond your reach — both personal and societal.

Final Words on Creativity:

Creativity and changing your life carefully are both relevant and reliant on one another. When you face changes in your lifestyle, sometimes the only way to get through it is to approach your situation with creativity. A creative mindset will alter how you respond to a given situation or problem. The change in your life and the creativity you must tap into in order to deal with it will threaten your status quo and shift you in a new direction. You may encounter stress after stress, but simultaneously, you will experience joy and enjoyment with a creative mind.

Sometimes, these changes can happen too quickly. Too much change in our lifestyle can cause us to suffer anxiety. There are certain boundaries that limit and affect our ability to recover from rapid changes and come to a point of restoration in our lives. We must devote some time to addressing these issues. While we may experience a powerful surge of inspiration to make certain changes, and we may have the perseverance to do so and be recognized for it, there are also similarly powerful hang-ups against making those changes.

Changes of this magnitude need creativity and alternative thinking on the part of everyone involved, including loved ones. Life's just one change after another, but this change is what allows us to develop and evolve as human beings.

Like it or not, change will occur to you. And once you notice that this normal characteristic of life is unavoidable and should not be scary, you will become a more improved person; since there is always room for improvement. Maybe a significant lifestyle change has occurred to you already; maybe not. But you can't prevent it. Actually, it is simpler if you accept the change rather than fight against it. When you do, you can use your creativity to your benefit. Since creativity is the key to achievement. Consider once again the innovative reflection discussed previously in this chapter. Relax slowly, and drop right in. We have all been there, or we will be there eventually. It is not what happens to you in life that matters; it is how you *manage* what happens that makes a difference. It is how you allow your innovative mind to cope with the issues at hand that affects your outcome. Everything you encounter in life will change you in some way. If you do not agree with and accept these changes, then you are not agreeing with and accepting yourself. This is because all of life's changes carry new and higher goals for you to attain, making you smarter as time moves along. Preventing these changes would actually diminish who you are. Life isn't just about discovering. Life is also about developing.

To maintain your developing creativity, everything needs to be in position. Balance is the key term. The issue is there in front of you, along with the necessary abilities you need to address it. You know you can do it. You are loaded with self- confidence. Creative power fills up the space within you. Everything just clicks into place. It is the ideal environment for problem solving. Remember, you are not alone, and as more individuals engage in this procedure, the more power there is for all.

When your creative power is in its fullest expression and you know your abilities are equal to the task at hand, this is known as the "white moment." It is when everything comes together harmoniously. This is often called being "in the zone." When someone is in the zone, he or she can't do anything incorrect. Her abilities are so well equal to whatever it is she is accomplishing that it almost seems as though the two are working together as one.

However, you will be able to determine if something is not right for you at this time in your life, or if your abilities are not up to the task. You will experience nervousness and be afraid of failing. If for some reason your abilities far exceed the situation you are in, you will become tired and unsettled. This is an indicator that you are generally not using your skills to your benefit. You need more of a challenge.

In conclusion, we need a more "Zen" no-mind time to engage in whatever creative activities we choose. We need to make a more Zen-like environment within our home. Nothing is more invigorating than being "in the zone," or arriving at the "white moment," Allowing freedom in your life to discover moments when you can slide out of your power and into a more Zen-like state of no-mind. Appreciate your ideas. Appreciate fixing those problems or dilemmas and placing them behind you.

References

Ameriplan. (2011, September). Various medical plans for families and individuals. http://www.ameriplanusa.com

Annual Credit Report. (2012). Free Credit Report Once a Year. http://www.annualcreditreport.com

Modest Needs. (2012). Grant Assistance for Individuals Needing Help with Bills. http://www.modestneeds.org

Patient Services Incorporated. (2012, October). Medical Assistance. http://www.patientservicesinc.org

Safe Link Wireless. (2012). Free Cell Phone for Income Eligible Families. http://www.safelinkwireless.com

Social Security. (2012). Disability. http://www.socialsecurity.gov

Turmeric Powder. (2010). Uses of Turmeric Powder. www.tumeric.com

United States Department of Labor. (2011. April). The Fair Labor Standards Act. http://www.dol.gov

Ways to Work. (2010). Provide a loan for income-eligible families to purchase a car. http://www.waystowork.org

CoAbode. (2011). Single Mothers Sharing Housing. http://www.coabode.com

Credit Kharma. (2012). Review Credit Report Information for free, literally.

Retrieved from http://www.creditkharma.com

Free Charity Cars. (2011). Give free Cars. Retrieved from http://www.freecharitycars.org

Grall, T. S. (2010, February). Custodial Mothers and Father and their Child

Support. Retrieved from http://www.census.gov/prod/2009/pubs/p60- 237.pdf

Habitat of Humanity. (2012). Home ownership for low-to moderate income families. Retrieved from http://www.habitat.org

Health Well Foundation. (2012, September). Medical Assistance for Individuals with Certain Diseases. Retrieved from http://www.healthwellfoundation.org

Job Corps. (2012). Helping Young Adults into the Workforce. Retrieved from http://www.jobcorps.com

Lexington Law. (2012). Fix Credit Report. Retrieved from http://www.lexingtonlaw.com

Index

everyday, *45-47, 49*

everyone, *42, 46, 52*

everything, *21, 43, 52-53*

Everywhere, *21*

evidence, *7*

evolve, *52*

exactly, *26, 29, 33, 46, 48*

exam, *8*

example, *25, 34, 50*

exceed, *53*

excellence, *43*

excellent, *16-17, 28, 30, 40*

excess, *21*

excited, *38*

exciting, *37*

exclusive, *9*

exclusively, *7*

exempt, *12*

exercise, *34, 36-37, 47*

exhausted, *16, 34*

exist, *50*

existence, *43-44*

expectant, *12*

expectation, *47*

Expected, *22*

expecting, *11*

expense, *18*

expenses, *21, 28*

experience, *7, 11, 14, 44, 49, 51, 53*

experienced, *41*

experiences, *3, 33*

expert, *42*

expired, *29*

Exposed, *4, 21*

expressing, *46*

expression, *49, 53*

Extending, *37*

extra, *7, 12, 14, 21, 23*

extract, *34-35*

extraneous, *37*

extravagant, *45*

extremely, *9, 11, 19, 31, 43*

eyes, *33*

F

face, *25, 40, 47, 51*

facility, *14*

fact, *27*

factor, *47, 50*

FAFSA, *22-23*

failing, *50, 53*

Fair, *12, 54*

fall, *51*

familiar, *31, 37*

Families, *54*

families, *15, 54-55*

Family, *9, 22*

family, *8, 14-16, 18, 33*

fantastic, *48*

far, *20, 25, 43, 53*

fascinates, *25*

fast, *12*

Father, *55*

father, *8-9, 14, 28*

fathers, *6-7*

features, *34-36*

February, *55*

federal, *12, 20-23*

fee, *17, 19, 22, 30*

feel, *30, 33-34, 46, 50*

feeling, *23, 45*

feelings, *34, 36, 48*

fees, *22*

J

M

U

W

22244106R00048

Made in the USA
Lexington, KY
18 April 2013